Ed. 344

G. Schirmer's Editions
of
Oratorios and Cantatas

—

HYMN OF PRAISE

A Sacred Cantata

For Full Chorus of Mixed Voices
Three Solo Voices (Two Sopranos and Tenor)
with Piano Accompaniment

by

FELIX MENDELSSOHN

ISBN 978-0-7935-4709-8

G. SCHIRMER, Inc.

DISTRIBUTED BY
HAL•LEONARD®
CORPORATION
7777 W. BLUEMOUND RD. P.O. BOX 13819 MILWAUKEE, WI 53213

INDEX

Hymn of Praise

Lobgesang

Nº 1. Sinfonia

Felix Mendelssohn-Bartholdy

Printed in the U.S.A. by G. Schirmer, Inc.

A Allegro (♩ = 160)

IV

X

Maestoso con moto *(come prima)*

Allegretto un poco agitato (♩.=80)

Adagio religioso (♪ = 76)

HYMN OF PRAISE.

(LOBGESANG.)
CANTATA.
(CHORUS.)

№ 1.

F. Mendelssohn Bartholdy, Op. 52.

Allegro moderato maestoso. (M.=100.)

4

8

5187

10

"PRAISE THOU THE LORD."

(Solo and Chorus.)

Nº 2.

Molto più moderato ma con fuoco. (♩ = 104.)

great loving kind - ness. Praise thou the Lord, O my spir - it, and for-get thou

not, and for-get thou not, for-get thou not all His ben - e -fits. Praise thou the

Praise thou the

Praise thou the

Praise thou the

Praise thou the

my in-most soul praise His kindness, His great lov - ing kind - ness, Praise His

kindness, His great lov - ing kind - ness, Praise thou the Lord, Praise thou the Lord,

Praise thou the Lord, Praise thou the Lord.

Praise thou the Lord, Praise thou the Lord.

Praise thou the Lord, Praise thou the Lord.

Praise thou the Lord, Praise thou the Lord,

20

5187

"SING YE PRAISE."

(RECIT.)

№ 3.

"ALL YE THAT CRIED UNTO THE LORD."

(Chorus.)

Nᵒ 4.

"I WAITED FOR THE LORD."

(DUET AND CHORUS.)

Nº 5.

36

5187

38

5187

"THE SORROWS OF DEATH."

(SOLO.)

Nº 6.

—from the dead, and a-wake thou that sleep-est, and a-wake, thou that sleepest,

I bring thee sal-va-tion. The

sor-rows of death had clos-ed all a-round me, and Hell's dark-terrors

had got hold up-on me, with troub-le and deep heav-i-ness, with

troub-le and deep heav-i-ness. But, said the Lord, Come, a-

rise, come, a - rise_____ from the dead, and a - wake thou that

sleep-est, and a - wake thou that sleep-est! I bring thee sal - va -

tion, I bring thee sal - va -

B Allegro assai agitato. ($\flat$ = 84.) RECIT.

tion. We call - ed thro' the

dark - ness, Lento. Watchman, will the night soon pass?_____

Watchman, will the night soon pass?___ The Watch - man on - ly

said: Though the morn-ing will come, the night will come al - so;

Ask ye en - quire ye, ask if ye will, en - quire ye, re - turn a -

gain, ask: Watchman, will the night soon pass?___

Watchman, will the night soon pass?___ The Watch - man on - ly

"THE NIGHT IS DEPARTING."

(CHORUS.)

N°7.

Allegro maestoso e molto vivace.(♩.= 96.)

56

5187

"LET ALL MEN PRAISE THE LORD."

(CHORALE.)

№ 8.

62

"MY SONG SHALL BE ALWAY THY MERCY."

(DUET.)

Nº 9.

64

5187

66

5187

"YE NATIONS, OFFER TO THE LORD."

(CHORUS.)

Nº 10.

5187

78

5187

80

5187